I0149261

Los Quotes has been designed so that each page can be hung up as a friendly reminder, or given to someone you feel can use a kind word of encouragement.

Let's build a community through positivity.

LOVE IS ALL NU NEED

PROPULSION

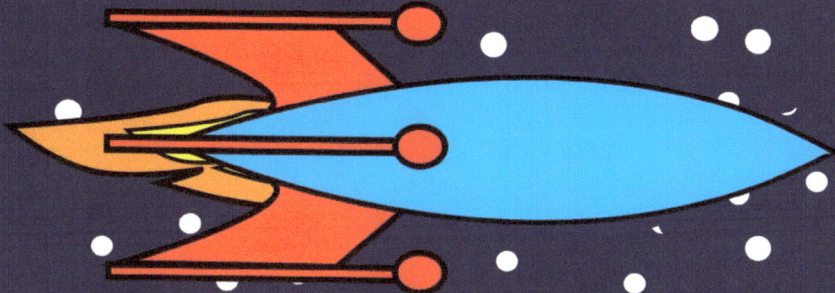

USE ANY OPPOSITION
TO YOUR HAPPINESS,
AS FUEL TO PROPEL
YOU INTO THE LIFE
YOU ENVISION!

ESPADA ART
WWW.LOSESPADA.COM

EVEN THE STRONG, NEED A SHOULDER!

ESPADA ART

www.losespada.com

LOS ESPADA ART

WWW.LOSESPADA.COM

MY MIND IS NEVER SILENT !

ESPADA ART

WWW.LOSESPADA.COM

TIME DOES NOT EXIST WHEN AN ARTIST IS CREATING!!

BE YOURSELF!

THE MOMENT YOU STOP WORRYING ABOUT THE PUBLIC OPINION, IS THE DAY YOU DISCOVER

FREEDOM!

ART HAS NO RULES OR GUIDE LINES. IT'S WHAT YOU MAKE IT. OTHERS DO NOT HAVE TO GET IT, AS LONG AS IT MAKES YOU **HAPPY!**

GET YOURS!

ESPADA
ART

WWW.LOSESPADA.COM

NOTHING CAN STOP A DETERMINED HEART

ESPADA ART

WWW.LOSESPADA.COM

SPREAD LOVE,
JOY AND INSPIRATION!
THE WORLD ALREADY
HAS A GOOD GRIP ON
SADNESS, HATE AND
NEGATIVITY!

ESPADA ART
www.losespada.com

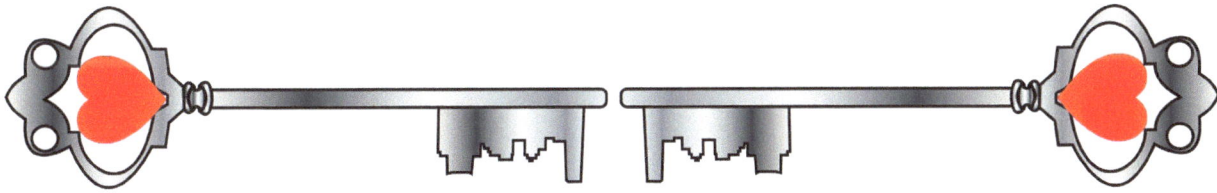

THE KEYS TO YOUR NEW LIFE ARE READY! ARE YOU?

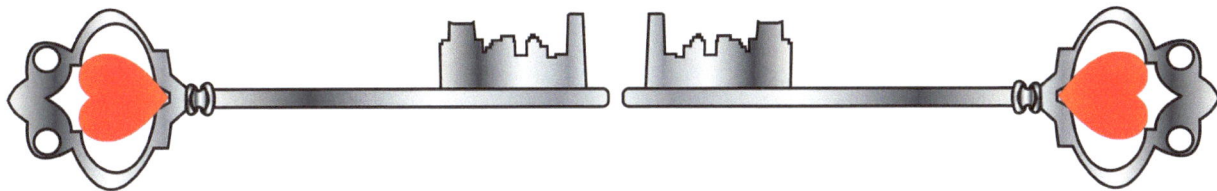

ESPADA ART
WWW.LOSESPADA.COM

WHEN WAS THE LAST TIME YOU LIVED FOR YOU?

ESPADA ART
WWW.LOSESPADA.COM

DO NOT WAIT FOR PERMISSION TO
LIVE!

SMILE AND SING!
IT'S GOING TO BE
OK!

MAKE YOUR PATH!!
WHEN YOU PLACE RULES IN FRONT OF CREATIVITY, YOU LIMIT YOURSELF!

ESPADA ART

WORK SO HARD, THAT YOUR HEROES BECOME YOUR PEERS!

ESPADA ART

www.losespada.com

WHEN YOU CHOOSE TO NO LONGER SETTLE DUE TO LONELINESS. THE RIGHT PERSON WILL EARN YOUR HEART.

COMFORTABLE SILENCE, SPEAKS VOLUMES

THE GREATEST THING YOU CAN WEAR TODAY?

A SMILE!

STAY DRIVEN!

THE MOMENT YOU LOSE FOCUS, YOU LOSE SELF!

RESPECT
THE GRIND!
YOU CAN NOT GO FROM
A-Z
WITHOUT TRIPPING OVER THE REST OF THE ALPHABET!

What's on the other side of

FEAR?

LIFE

LOVE

REWARDS

SATISFACTION

ACHIEVEMENT

SUCCESS

ENDLESS POSSIBILITIES!

ESPADA ART

www.losespada.com

THE MIND OF AN ARTIST IS ONE OF MANY WONDERS

www.losespada.com

IF ALL YOU SEE ARE ROADBLOCKS, YOU'LL NEVER REACH YOUR GOALS!..

9 780692 756539